CW00418988

For me, for her; and all of those who shared their time reminding me that even in the vastness of space, stars still pierce the sky to give light.

Table of Contents:

PANIC ATTACKS

I can't find the words to describe how it can feel sometimes but that doesn't mean I should stay silent to the fact that I am feeling like a used car that has been left on the side of the road to rust away.

I may feel like I'm drowning at the bottom of a bottle or like my feet are endlessly falling over each other like the words that fail to break through my lips because the tanks are empty.

That doesn't mean it's not okay. It's okay to feel nothing, or everything at one. It doesn't mean you're worthless or godlike in any way. It means you're human and you feel like any other thinking, feeling, breathing creature does as we cling to this tiny planet spinning through space.

What's not okay is if you constantly feel the weight and refuse to seek refuge from the constant grey cloud following overhead. It's not okay for others to label mental illness like a DVD stuck on repeat with the same old names and reasons and whys.

Why am I like this? Why is this happening to me? Why can't anyone see me?

The throat burns with each drink. I can feel my bones within my skin, and it itches like every scar. I'm not the only one feeling eyes on the back of their neck. Looks of an inability to have the compassion or love to try to understand when all we want is

an embrace, a glimpse of care, an open hand.

But with each glance or day where it feels like the world is both motionless and racing, I believe, like a morning spring, life builds and moves, and we grow. Eventually the sun stays out

longer and longer until the clouds fade away.
There's nothing wrong with helping it grow. Using
medicine like soil and words like oxygen.

Everything will be okay.

KITCHEN SINK

how long will I stay gasping for air,

body sinking,

further and further,

beneath the waves...

my fingertips are all that are left

above water.

You've touched my hand so many times

but each time I hope I'm taken to shore,

I'm baptised.

I drown.

PAVEMENTS

I'm trapped between the cracks in the pavement

feeling like borrowed space.

I can't breathe. It's confusion.

I'm floating in a sky of deafening silence with

waves of still noise crashing overhead.

I can't hold the pressure in my chest like the

engine stalled and the mechanic got lost on the

way.

I can't see the exit signs on the backs of my hands.

I can't breathe.

There's too much traffic in my mind.

SOLAR WINDS

my biggest question isn't to do with some
omnipotent force that circles most people's lives
like a constant ellipsis, punctuating every thought
into existence.

I wonder about why we are so self-destructive and
why inflicting pain on ourselves and others can
somehow feel good.

people like to paint nothingness as a giant black
hole swallowing and all-consuming, but justifiably
sparked into reality when the night sky has
collapsed in its own inevitable grieving.

nothingness isn't like that at all.

the difference between a black hole and a void, is
that one has meaning whilst the other is
disregarded as just feelings.

EXCOMMUNICATED

It's the fact that I thought I couldn't communicate because every other conversation feels prerequisite and scripted.

But with you I speak with my soul, with such conviction, from the tongue to my teeth, to my eyes, to my ears.

I say I know so much whilst knowing so little.

There's so much I cannot fathom yet I'm self-assured, satisfied and smitten.

I'm your living, breathing, antiquated progressor professing no little, no less, it's all you.

VACUUM

It's weird to me that you joked about me being like the moon and the moon goes through a constant cycle of phases. You blamed me for the typhoon that consumed you whilst blistered with sun burns that kissed your skin from the nights you laid with them. We both revolved around you with your centre of gravity weighing us down and then you had the audacity to blame both day and night for the toxins in your atmosphere that you left us breathing in.

MARIONETTE

Sometimes I think I'm made of clay, but my maker forgot to shape me into a fully formed being. So as a little puppet, I let other people play with my strings.

No mask can hide the lies in a forced smile and inability to look you in the eyes.

My nose is an olive branch.

Leaf an outreached hand.

LIFE-SIZED

sometimes life feels like cardboard,

people feel like placeholders as the thread that sews

people together are constantly worn to a thin line that

breaks, tangles or is cut.

I feel like safety scissors testing the strength of each string,

because I can't find meaning in the fistful of

intertwined wool now dancing in my palm.

MELTDOWN

There is something about the way the world speaks

in both bellows and whispers that leaves the

defences stood at attention stationed side by side

defenceless.

They writhe and weave and squeeze without

reprieve until surrounded.

Raised hairs, raised fingertips, too late.

The smallest echo, now a relentless trojan invading

my every essence.

The rising scream from within is deafening

drowning all other entrance at the gate

burning me alive from the inside.

Gasping in all the air around me until its

extinguished

stamping down the rising, like makeshift whack a

mole,

final breath, eyes open, steady,

sound again.

MINDFUL

Feeling both futility and infinity all at once.

Balanced in a way I imagine those who say they

found God, meaning or another

profound profit.

Feeling everything all at once, both endless

magnitude and microscopic atoms.

Interconnected as if she speaks, "wake up, open

your eyes."

Whole, found.

Sinking deep into the velvet sky of the universe.

Wide awake, listening.

Fear, doubt inexplicably vacate my nature.

crepuscular rays cut through the nimbus and rain

traces my cheeks.

Scattered, golden, sparkling hues.

I am alive, I exist.

INVISIBLE

I already feel alien and then my own bones reject
me

I'm not exactly sad or angry yet, just exhausted

but you can't be exhausted when running on
adrenaline

but you can't be in pain when running on anything

I get pins and needles just from sitting one way

too long, too still, don't move, do move, can't win

It isn't bad enough or to the point of needing
braces

so I brace myself for the onslaught of we don't do
preventative

It's normal for your body to make that grinding and
snap

It's normal for your chest to feel as though it might

explode

It's normal for your skin to crawl and race after a

menial task

It's normal, your normal, the tests say so

oh actually no, I don't understand how you're able

to stand

but there's not a thing I can do to make sure that

lasts

you're just going to have to get used to it

you're just going to have to get used to it

meds wear off too fast and will screw up your

insides

you're just so strong and were built for this fight

they will call you hypochondriac on the days you
panic

and call you a liar on the days you point out its
chronic

I try so hard not to be a pessimist when thorns
pierce my skin

I've settled on cynical

I give out my good and try to find silver linings

I'm kind to myself and try to just fully live

because I was terrified of everything before I had a
reason

no one wanted to listen so I just stopped speaking

my entire insides can move out of place

they could get the type wrong or develop a co-
morbidity

nah it's all in your head, even if on paper,

it's just hormones or general anxiety

I don't want pity or painkillers or well wishing

I wanna be seen and listened to, believed without

asking to be

but then on other days just don't perceive me

I was already invisible then my body decided to

join me

NIGHTSCAPE

There is a strange comfort in the stillness of the

City at night.

The deepest ocean of the sky is a blanket of

constellations, infinite universes, possibilities all

taking place at once.

When daylight spills, its brash, its blinding, its

concrete business suits rushing, impatient, no, I

prefer the night.

Reality is altered in the shapes of skyscrapers like

the gaps, the hidden spaces, small moments before

page turning.

Whether its the final chapter of a really long good

story or a breath of air after a heavy weight,

gasping, suffocating.

But dusk comes again and it's all okay. The corner

where time freezes and tomorrow is anything and

could be anything you want it to be.

CHRONIC

and I know my self-worth, I don't hate myself, I

hate the world,

perpetual teenage angst cos they fed my woes to

the fat cats,

sing to me sweetly another chorus of lame excuses

stripped of substance,

If I hear another mantra about yoga and meditation

you're gonna find yourself picking out your teeth

off of the pavement.

don't tell me to be patient, when I'm proverbially

the patient,

prescribed to prescribe to a fixation on fictitious

medications,

I'm vexed at the facade you facilitate whilst

spitting fake remedies,

whilst I spit it out loud, fidelity to a chemically

induced necropsy.

my worn-out spine and underlined pages are slave

to the system,

so tell me what the hell am I supposed to do with

this one?

Tell me that its only temporary when the

symptoms are persistent,

then in the next line tell me how they are all non-

existent.

GOOD GRIEF

I mourn the future that I'll never have, not the life
I've lived.
I punish myself for the days I've wasted.
I choke on the words at the back of my throat
because I can't form them into full sentences
I want this. I need that.

I don't know how to ask when I never asked for
this. I never wanted this.
Caught between toxic positivity and self-
deprecation, I'm humbled.
I know most of the time what I want and how to
obtain that, but when I'm floored
and on my knees, all I feel is like an anchor that's
trying to tread water.
I don't push away; I try to pull closer.

But I know there isn't a ring you can throw out that
would make it easier.

No one can fight or feel this but me.

I'm trying to tell my body to stop fighting itself.

I have no control and everything aches,

and then my chest aches,

and then my mind aches.

I can't ask you for reassurance about how you feel

because I still feel it here.

I can't ask you to hold me because I know right

now, you can't be near.

I can't ask you to tell me it's okay or it's going to

be when the pain doesn't disappear.

I want a day off. I want respite.

But even if I beg with everything in me to feel well

rested in this moment, it won't come.

I have to be patient and wait for it to lessen but not

to leave.

I want to find the words and speak, but it's just so

hard when I'm already having to remind

myself, how to breathe or still believe.

EVERGREEN

I stare out at space

because I find the reminder of gravity to be

grounding.

Like my feet sink into the earth beneath me

and grow roots bending through to the lithosphere.

My arms are branches,

my ribs a nest for the soul at home in my chest.

The pith at my centre is a forget-me-not.

Constant like the changing of seasons,

I stand, I stay, I grow.

SWIMMING LESSONS

You warned me that you were raging fires,
my arrogance was that I believed that I wouldn't
get burned.
You warned me that you were the storming ocean,
and now I can feel myself sinking and sinking
below waves.

I need to let you find your own calmness and
stillness
before I enter this place as I did before. I know you
will.
Showing up and being present because you want
to, that is real love.

BRANDED

Your fingertips mark my soul, intertwined,

linen lace delicately bruised,

thoughtfully, carefully, consciously,

your eyes spark embers that glisten ferociously,

no man-made stone or crystal crafted by earth

could compare,

lips that partition to release sweet songs

that although you cannot hear,

make sparrows weep.

Oceans could not contain the delicate features of

your soul.

Forgive me for I am a thief,

I desire to steal every moment, every whisper,

every heartbeat.

Your roots ensnare my ribs and burrow into my

spine, like hands embracing in gentle prayer.

Like mountains you move me, enrapture me, my

love, my all, without fear.

MOONBEAMS

My love is warm,

it isn't phased by thunders or monsoons,

no tidal wave could make me move,

only I would move these mountains with words,

or these hands, or my soul,

if you asked me to I would try,

with toolbox in hand to pull the moon

from the sky so that your ocean didn't

have to be unsettled by the changing of tides.

But there is no malice in the moon,

she only wishes to prevail the winds and valleys,

to fill the spaces on our curved trajectory,

A great force to be reckoned with or

hushed humming with open arms widespread

I would kiss your wounds softly and

remind you of who I see, of what I perceive,

even if you sometimes can't see or speak or

believe,

chew my ears down to the shining core of me,

they stopped being only mine the moment I
became we.

BITTERSWEET

Nothing exists but this in its echoes, ripple out
amongst my inner workings.
Like you somehow exist in every memory of what
is, what was, what will be.
I feel both endless and bound by your glow,
glistening that both blinds and binds you.
If I am but a pen, you are the ink that caresses
every page and signs every letter knowingly
yet deftly, powerfully apt.
Sweet Reckoning.
Each letter punctuated through palms meeting,
fingers folded, both needed and pressed into the
page.
Oh what sweet bliss! to sign the edges with our
names entangled.
Like freckles, blotted calligraphy stains the corner
of every verse of the never-ending volume we play
tennis with.

Stubborn courage philosophy met with eager
encouragement.

Silence meeting sound.

SALTWATER

your love is like a tidal wave,

I stood on the edge afraid to let you in,

but your current pulled me into the ocean.

now I am left to sink into saltwater,

whilst watching your form taking shape at the

shore.

you planted seeds in my chest that bloomed,

and grew and grew and grew,

but then one day you stopped watering them.

RELINQUISH

being alive is consistent death and rebirth,

old cells vacate our form, we shed our skins,

our mind tries to hold on to ideas and expectations,

whilst life will tell us to start living over existence,

stop looking for answers because truth is no one

has them,

true freedom comes within by letting go of

attachment.

HAUNTED

it's funny how after learning how to give myself
basic affection,
that my inner workings would start to crave
deconstruction,
strip me down to my barest parts,
a core of a ghost with a beating heart,
I would be seeking out attention, villainized,
but just a kid staring out from a crescent cradle,
maybe if I fit as the idealized daughter,
maybe I would worry less about who I'd grow to
be in future,
inner conflict between self-love or perceiving
myself as a narcissist,
inner conflict between being told there's something
wrong vs development
of a victim complex,
Roles reversed, barman, friend and therapist,
but when it came down to it, down to the second,
no one rushed to my side when the axis was tilted,

or to see, hear, celebrate what truly mattered,

or I guess what only mattered to me,

and I now struggle to share that or let it in,

or I find the need to overcompensate,

What I am, What I am, What am I?

a constant balancing act,

started depending on myself when I became the
supportive friend,

because I felt galaxies away from a support system
on which I could depend,

the polarity is the naive part of me believing in
change because I have seen it,

I hold so much faith and so much hope, even in the
midst of learning to let it go.